CLOISTER

BOOKS

Cloister Books are inspired by the monastic custom of reading as one walks slowly in the monastery cloister—a place of silence, centering, and calm. Within these pages you will find a similar space in which to pray and reflect on the presence of God.

COWLEY PUBLICATIONS is a ministry of the brothers of the Society of Saint John the Evangelist, a monastic order in the Episcopal Church. Our mission is to provide books and resources for those seeking spiritual and theological formation. COWLEY PUBLICATIONS is committed to developing a new generation of writers and teachers who will encourage people to think and pray in new ways about spirituality, reconciliation, and the future.

Remember Your Baptism

Remember Your Baptism

৺

Ten Meditations

Jeanne Finan

Cowley Publications
Cambridge, Massachusetts

Library of Congress Cataloging-in-Publication Data:
Finan, Jeanne, 1949-
    Remember your baptism : ten meditations / Jeanne Finan.
        p. cm.
Includes bibliographical references.
    ISBN 1-56101-273-4 (pbk.: alk. paper) 1. Baptism—Meditations.
    I.Title.
BV811.3.F56 2005
234'.161—dc22

                          2004026645

Scripture quotations are taken from the New Revised Standard Version of the Bible, © 1989, by the Division of Christian Education of the National Council of the Churches of Christ in the United States of America. Used by permission.

"At Blackwater Pond" by Mary Oliver. Copyright © 1992 by Mary Oliver. From *New and Selected Poems*, Beacon Press. Used with the permission of the Molly Malone Cook Literary Agency.

Cover Design: Jennifer Hopcroft
Text Design: Lindy Gifford
Illustrations by Charles Perkalis

This book was printed in the United States of America on acid-free paper.

Cowley Publications
4 Brattle Street
Cambridge, Massachusetts 02138
800-225-1534 • www.cowley.org

For my parents
Mary and Jack

Acknowledgments 11

Introduction 14

1 Sacrament 18

2 Water 28

3 Chrism 42

4 Spirit 52

5 Do You? Will You? 58

6 Covenant 64

7 Communion 72

8 Witness 78

9 Welcome! 86

10 Remember Your Baptism 90

Notes 95

Acknowledgments

This manuscript had a wonderful and joyful beginning as an independent study while I was a student at Virginia Theological Seminary. Could anyone have a better faculty advisor that Bishop Mark Dyer? I don't think so. He offered his wisdom and encouragement and, to my surprise (and delight), he insisted that these meditations needed to be read by more people than just the two of us. Thanks to Bishop Mark these meditations found their way into an envelope and off in the mail to Cowley Publications.

I am also very grateful to:

⅋ Brother Kevin Hackett for his early encouragement and enthusiasm and to Michael Wilt for his continuing encouragement and perceptive recognition that I am a person who needs deadlines.

❧ Mitzi Budde for her careful and discerning reading of this manuscript in its early stages, her many helpful suggestions and her keen eye for split infinitives

❧ Danby Ludgate, friend and artist, who helped me create prayer cloths for each of these meditations. What a fun and fine time that was!

❧ The Reverend Doug Bailey, who invited me on the journey that first opened my heart to God's grace

❧ To the Right Reverend Robert H. Johnson, my bishop during the time of these writings, who offered encouragement for my writing as well as my priesthood

❧ The women of the Diocesan ECW board of Western North Carolina, who, while on retreat at the Valle Crucis Conference Center, graciously listened to a reading of my first draft of these meditations

❧ Liz Ward for her patient and holy direction

❧ David, Susan, Nanese, Kevin, Glenda, Vickie, and Bill, who have collectively held me together with prayer, even in times when there wasn't much left of me to hold together

℘ The Reverend Rick Lawler, Beth Postlethwait, Bill Stroh, and all the people of St. Mary of the Hills, Blowing Rock, who make every day a wondrous adventure into the mystery of God's love

℘ and most especially to my family, Tom and Benares and Jody and Natalie and Cedar and Garth: wild things, you make my heart sing!

Introduction

The idea for these mediations began after attending a prebaptismal counseling session at the church where I was doing an internship as a seminarian. Even though the priest was warm and welcoming and the adults, parents, and sponsors were excited, something seemed to be missing from the short lecture accompanied by a few points written on a flip chart. Are we really conveying the depth and beauty of the sacrament of baptism, I wondered? Might there be a better way to prepare people? Of course, some parishes have a long catechumenal process before baptism, but I wasn't looking for more information. I was looking for a way to help people become more spiritually centered as they prepared for the day of their baptism or their child's baptism.

I also began to think back to my own baptism.

Having grown up in the Baptist Church, I was baptized at age eleven by full immersion. I have vivid memories of my white robe floating on top of the water as I walked toward the minister. I even remember the moment of fretting about that floating robe, worrying that the congregation, much to my dismay, was going to get a pew-side view of my underpants! Sadly, I also remember feeling disappointed when I came up from under the water and there were no doves or angels or great rays of light shining down upon me. Where was that voice booming out, "You are my beloved . . ."? My childhood theological roots were in literalism, not sacramentalism. Thinking back, I realize that neither my church nor my family had prepared me for baptism. I don't say this to blame, but rather to reflect that my own baptism memories also affirm a need for addressing the spiritual meaning of baptism. I believe this need crosses the lines of denomination and age. But as parents or as individuals, we do not necessarily know how to do this.

As I continued to pray about this, I realized

that I was not looking for a new Christian education curriculum on preparation for baptism, but for a way that we might continue to prayerfully ponder our baptism and the baptism of our children. I felt a need to develop a means, humble as it may be, to create a small window of time and space in one's life to consider the ongoing meaning of baptism for our lives. As a result of these wonderings and out of my own deep longing, I have written this series of meditations about baptism.

I have attempted to write these meditations to bring people into *kairos* time, rather than fitting baptism into the *chronos* time of our busy lives. I wrote these meditations to help move the reader or listener into a slow-motion dance with God and sacramentality.

These meditations can be used as individual introductions for more in-depth prebaptismal sessions, or all ten could be used together in one longer session, for prebaptismal counseling, for a retreat with those considering baptism, or for those who are already baptized.

The meditations might also serve as personal meditations for individuals: those considering their own baptism, or those, as parents, who desire baptism for their baby or their child. My hope is that these meditations are meaningful beyond pre-baptismal reflection and are valuable in helping us remember our own baptism, either literally or metaphorically, moving us into a deeper understanding of this great sacrament given by Christ to his Church.

Baptism is completely free, but it will cost you everything.

The voice of God in the burning bush is the sacrament that forever changes Moses.

1

ༀ

Sacrament

*Let us now pray for these persons who are
to receive the Sacrament of new birth.*

(*Book of Common Prayer [BCP]*, 305)

As Christians, we believe
that baptism is one of the sacraments given to us by
Jesus Christ. What does that mean? What do we
mean by the word s*acrament*? If we turn to the Cate-
chism in the *Book of Common Prayer,* we learn that
"sacraments are outward and visible signs of inward
and spiritual grace, given by Christ as sure and certain means by which we receive that grace" (857).
To put it another way, God uses our surrounding
physical world—the common, human world we

live in every day, our outer and visible world of space and time and matter—to mysteriously reach out and touch our inner world, our soul. When outward and inward meet and embrace, we are showered with God's divine grace.

Sacraments are vibrant and multidimensional; nothing about a sacrament is flat or one-dimensional. Center yourself on these two dimensions of a sacrament: the outer sign of the sacrament and the inner effect of the sacrament. Sacraments are the simultaneous happening of the seen and the unseen.

The outer sign is the seen; it is the visible, human-created but God initiated element. The outward and visible sign is God's guarantee, a promise to be present and tangibly real for us. We are physical people, and like Thomas, we lean toward doubt unless we have physical evidence. We need that tangible, active dimension as our cue that God is on the move in the world.

The unseen dimension is God's grace actively and continuously at work in our lives. God is always there, but in the busyness of our lives, it is easy for us to miss or to take for granted God's presence. Sacraments are God's reveille for getting our spiritual attention.

It is the outer sign, the seen action, that initially captures our attention. It is the outward and visible sign that opens our senses to what is happening inside—both inside us and inside the sacrament itself. The outward and visible sign swings open the sacred door to our inward experience of the spiritual grace of the sacrament.

The inner effect is the true significance of what is happening. God uses the outward and visible signs to reach out to us and reveal to us the inward and spiritual grace of God. We may see only what is happening in the outward signs and symbols; but the important work of God is taking place inside us, in our deepest places. A sacrament is God's calling out loud, as Jesus did to the deaf mute in Mark's Gospel, "Ephphatah," that is, "Be opened" (Mark 7:34). Be opened to all that is really happening, to what you see and especially to what you cannot see.

A sacrament involves all the senses: we see, we

hear, we smell, we taste, we touch and feel. Think about that with baptism. We see the water in the font, the fire of the paschal candle, the baby held in the arms of the priest, the older child or adult as she or he steps to the font. We hear the sound of the splashing water, the words of the liturgy, the baptismal hymns. We smell the wax of the burning candles and the sweet smoke of incense. Our senses engage us, and even when we are only watching from the congregation, we, along with those being baptized, taste that single drop of water as it runs from forehead, down cheek, and to our lips. We feel the cool water as its deep wetness soaks into every pore of our being. We are never mere observers during the sacrament of baptism, for the sacrament totally absorbs us as God surrounds us and dances in every dimension.

Sacraments bind together our nonverbal and verbal worlds. By using symbols and actions together with words, our attention is directed beyond the mere physical world to the deep and invisible realities at the very heart of the sacrament.

In our baptism we encounter Christ, because Jesus is the original sacrament: "And the Word became flesh and lived among us" (John 1:14). Jesus came into the world as the outward and visible sign—that fully human, visible, historical, embodied Jesus—of the inward and spiritual grace of the fully divine God. Just as Christ was the sure and certain sign of God's grace, the sacrament of baptism is the sure and certain sign through which we receive that grace ourselves.

In baptism it is the outward and visible signs of the water of the bath and the oil of the chrism that reveal the inward and spiritual grace of the union with Christ in his death and Resurrection. The sacrament of baptism reveals our own birth into God's family, the Church. For some, part of the reality of the sacrament of baptism is the forgiveness of sin— our self-imposed sentence of separation from God—and the beginning of a new life in the Holy Spirit. Baptism is the sacrament by which we publicly proclaim our adoption as God's children and celebrate being claimed as Christ's own.

It is important to remember that the grace generously given and received in the sacrament of baptism is not ceremonial, but is fully and truly the grace of Jesus Christ. A sacrament is pure gift from pure God. The blessing is not accidental.

Sacrament is not a word you find anywhere in the Bible, yet scripture overflows with sacrament. Think about it. When God speaks to Moses in the burning bush on Mount Horeb, hearing the voice of God is the sacrament that forever changes the life of Moses (Exodus, chapter 3). The burning bush is the outward and visible sign. The voice of God is the outward and visible sign. But the inward and spiritual grace comes through the mystery of God's presence, not only in the bush at that moment but God's presence throughout Moses' life.

When Joshua sets up the twelve stones in a circle in Gilgal, he says to the Israelites:

When your children ask their parents in time to come, "What do these stones mean?" then you shall let your children know, "Israel crossed over the Jordan here on dry ground." (Joshua 4:21–22)

Those twelve stones are the symbol for the Israelites' freedom from bondage, the symbol of God's saving grace, God's "mighty hand," as Joshua praises. God has guided and stayed with the twelve tribes of Israel; God led the Israelites out of Egypt and over the Jordan, and their lives are changed forever.

Our baptism is a story we need to tell our children and our children's children.

Baptism is our sacrament and our symbol for freedom from bondage, the symbol of God's saving grace, of God's mighty hand that reaches out to claim us and change our lives forever.

And what about the woman who comes into the home of Simon the Pharisee and bathes the feet of Jesus with her tears (Luke 7:38)? Those tears are the sacrament of her extravagant and life-changing love for Jesus.

John baptizes Jesus in the River Jordan, and the sacramental sign of water initiates the ministry of Jesus (Mark, chapter 1).

Sacraments are our human encounter with God. Even though we do not always consciously notice the holy and mysterious that surrounds us, our entire world is truly God's sacrament. As Archbishop William Temple wrote, "We live in a sacramental universe." God is always there before we consciously arrive. Sacraments are not something we use to ring up God, to call God to come out and be momentarily present with us. Instead, sacraments open a sacred door to reveal to us the ever-present, holy God, who is already there and always waiting for us. When we open our eyes, our ears, our hearts, we stand on the holy ground of a sacramental moment, a sacred encounter. It is a moment when the fully human meets the fully divine.

Sacraments express the genuine mystery of God. They are not magical or superstitious acts, for everything that happens and is received comes through God's grace. Even though sacraments are part of the liturgical ceremony of the Church, they are not a performance and certainly not superfluous pomp. Sacraments are the truest and deepest of spiritual acts. Sacraments are not something done *to* a person, but something God invites us to receive.

God calls: "Lift up your hearts. Come. Follow me into the deep waters of divine mystery."

The intention of a sacrament is to reveal fully the true reality of one's life.

God swept over the face of the waters.

2

ॐ

Water

We thank you, Almighty God, for the gift of water.

(*BCP,* 306)

One of the most widely attested incidents in the life of Jesus is his baptism in the River Jordan by John the Baptist. All four gospel writers tell the story (Matthew 3:11, Mark 1:8, Luke 3:16, John 1:26). John spoke, "I baptize you with water." And with that baptism, Jesus' ministry began. It all started with water. Even the word *baptism* relates back to water, for *baptism* comes from a Greek word meaning "to dip" or "to plunge." The most profound outward and visible sign of the sacrament of baptism is the water.

It is interesting that you cannot find the word *sacrament* in the Bible, but you almost cannot avoid the word *water* in the Bible. The word *water* is mentioned 473 times, and that does not include references to streams, rivers, wells, springs, bathing, or washing. Water is everywhere.

From Genesis, when "God swept over the face of the waters" (1:2), to Noah and the flood (chapter 7), to the Israelites crossing through the Red Sea (Exodus, chapter 14), to the detailed purification rites in Leviticus and Numbers instructing how the Israelites "shall wash their clothes and bathe themselves in water and at evening they shall be clean," water is central. From Ezekiel, with God's promises to "sprinkle clean water upon you, and you shall be clean from all your uncleannesses" (36:25), to Jonah, who is cast into the seas with the waves and billows passing over him and the waters closing over him, water is power. The life-giving, life-taking images of water overflow from the Hebrew Scriptures.

Water is an ancient symbol for purification and cleansing. Judaism required those converting to the faith to bathe for purity. Throughout the Old Testament, there are mentions of ceremonial washing for purity and sanctification. As Psalm 51:2 says, "Wash me thoroughly from my iniquity, and cleanse me from my sin."

Water images continue into the New Testament scriptures. Jesus' first miracle is when he changes water into wine at the wedding in Cana (John 2:1–11). Water is the source and substance Jesus uses to transform, revealing who he truly is to his disciples. Here, as with baptism, the water is an outward and visible sign of the inward and spiritual grace.

The gospels give us a different twist on the Old Testament use of water as a symbol for purification and cleanliness. Water and washing become symbols of servanthood when Jesus also washes his disciples' feet:

And during supper Jesus, knowing that the Father had given all things into his hands, and that he had come from God and was going to God, got up from the table, took off his outer robe, and tied a towel around himself. Then he poured water into a basin and began to wash the

31

disciples' feet and to wipe them with the towel that was tied around him. He came to Simon Peter, who said to him, "Lord, are you going to wash my feet?" Jesus answered, "You do not know now what I am doing, but later you will understand." (John 13:2–7)

Through the love of God, the water of baptism moves us into servanthood to God and one another. When we come to the font, we are acclaiming that we come from God and will go to God. Even when we, like Simon Peter, do not understand everything completely and fully, Jesus still acts in our lives.

Water is a sign representing Christ's presence. When Jesus wants his disciples to be able to find him for the Passover meal, he uses water as a means for them to find their way: "Go into the city, and a man carrying a jar of water will meet you; follow him" (Mark 14:13). Through the waters of baptism, we, too, are led into Christ's presence.

Ironically, Pilate uses water to wash his hands in front of the crowd to prove that he is innocent of condemning Jesus to death (Matthew 27:24). Even the one who would flog Jesus and hand him over for crucifixion saw water as the great symbol of cleansing one's heart. Sadly, Pilate's water bath is the stagnant water of fear and denial and has no resemblance to "the river of the water of life, bright as crystal, flowing from the throne of God and of the Lamb" (Revelation 22:1), which bathes us at baptism.

Occasions of Jesus' healings are often accompanied by water. As part of the healing of the Gerasene demoniac, a herd of swine rush down a steep bank and drown in the waters of the sea (Mark 5:13). All that is holding us back is drowned. Death comes before life. When Jesus visits the pool in Bethzatha (John, chapter 5), he asks the sick man, "Do you want to be made well?" (5:6). The lame man believes the water in the pool has the power to heal him; Jesus must show him that it is not the water that has the power but God who possesses the power.

This is true in our baptismal waters as well. The power belongs to God, who works through the water. When we understand that Jesus' question "Do you want to be made well?" reaches far beyond our physical health, when we fully arrive at the

"Yes!" response to this question, we are indeed ready to wade in the water.

Even apart from the Bible, water plays a central role in the instruction of the early writings of the Christian faith. In the ancient Christian practices manual, *The Lord's Teaching through the Twelve Apostles*, there are very specific instructions for the use of water in baptism:

Having said all this beforehand, baptize in the name of the Father and of the Son and of the Holy Spirit, in running water.

If you do not have running water, however, baptize in another kind of water; if you cannot in cold, then in warm.

But if you have neither, pour water on the head thrice in the name of Father and Son and Holy Spirit.[1]

Cold. Warm. Running. Still. Deep. Shallow. The temperature, the movement, even the quantity of the water is unimportant. Just like the story of the rich man and Lazarus, "Have mercy on me, and send Lazarus to dip the tip of his finger in water" (Luke 16:24), even the tiniest bit of water is all that is needed to give new life.

Because water is indeed life giving. We build communities around bodies of water. Water serves as a boundary between peoples and lands. Water quenches our thirst and strengthens our bodies. In fact, scientists tell us that the proportion of water in our human bodies is greater than any other element present. For biblical writers, and for some of us today, water is precious because it is also scarce. Without water we will die. But water has meaning beyond our physical lives. Water is symbol and sacrament and metaphor. Our longing and thirst for water reflects our deep longing for God. As the psalmist writes:

As a deer longs for flowing streams,
so my soul longs for you, O God.
My soul thirsts for God,
for the living God.

Deep calls to deep.
(Psalm 42:1–2,7)

O God, you are my God, I seek you;
My soul thirsts for you;
my flesh faints for you,
as in a dry and weary land where there is no water.
(Psalm 63:1)

Water is life.

But water is also wild and uncontrollable and powerful and life taking. Waters roar and flood, wash away and destroy. Water drowns us. In our life journeys and in our faith journeys, we do not always walk beside still waters. Our lives are sometimes like the storm in Luke's gospel: "A windstorm swept down on the lake, and the boat was filling with water, and they were in danger" (Luke 8:23). There is good reason to hold water in awe. There is reason to plead with Jesus to calm the storm when we are tossed about at sea.

Water is death.

Even though our immediate image of baptism is usually, and rightfully, one of joy and delight, it is also important to recognize what comes before the joy and delight. There is also the darkness that water symbolizes. The deeper one dives beneath the waters of the sea, the darker and darker it becomes. All light is consumed. The farther one moves from the surface, the closer one moves to death. The waters of baptism follow that journey, moving us from darkness into light. It is Christ who is the light that shines and pulls us from the depths: "The light shines in the darkness, and the darkness did not overcome it" (John 1:5).

God guides us into and under the water, sometimes literally, sometimes metaphorically. Regardless, we must give up. We surrender. We stop breathing. We let go, if only for a few moments. As the water pours over our foreheads, we give ourselves, consciously or unconsciously, to God. It is a self-revealing moment, a moment of thanksgiving:

Lord, you have searched me and known me.

.   .   .   .   .   .

Even the darkness is not dark to you;
    the night is as bright as the day,
    for darkness is as light to you.
For it was you who formed my inward parts;
    you knit me together in my mother's womb.

37

I praise you, for I am fearfully and wonderfully made.
  Wonderful are your works;
that I know very well.
      (Psalm 139:1,12–14)

As parents, when we bring our child to the waters of the baptismal font, we do something that is even more courageous and daring than offering ourselves to God: We offer our child. We admit that there is something in life than we cannot give our child. Regardless of the immense love we feel for this small and precious human being, no matter how responsible and caring we are as parents, we come to realize that we are as helpless and powerless as the infant in our arms. It is not humanly possible, regardless of our efforts or our bank accounts, for us to give that sure and certain grace we desire for our children. In a sense we offer our child to die—so that our child might truly live. Even though infant baptism is not a requirement in the Episcopal faith tradition, we joyfully baptize young children because our heart's desire is that they might have life and have it abundantly from the very beginning of their lives.

There is a baptismal font at the Abbey Basilica of Maryhelp, at Belmont Abbey, outside of Charlotte, North Carolina. It is the first thing you see when you step into the narthex. The font is made from an enormous stone, a circular block of rough granite that has been hollowed out in one spot to create the font. The stone was originally used as a slave block; slaves stood on that very stone over one hundred years ago. On that stone, human beings were sold to the highest bidder. This same stone now serves as the baptismal font for the Basilica at Belmont Abbey. A plaque attached to the stone reads:

Upon this rock, men once were sold into slavery. Now upon this rock, through the waters of Baptism, men become free children of God.

To men and women, boys and girls, babes in arms, those of us who walk to the font, and those of us who are carried—the water of baptism offers freedom.

Baptism is more than a font and more than still, plain water sitting quietly. The water of baptism is living water: noisy, rushing, moving, pouring. It is water that does more than just wash us and cleanse us; it is a vital part of the outward and visible sign of God's revealed grace, the quenching of our deepest thirst.

Life-taking, life-giving water embraces us in the sacrament of baptism. We die with Christ and we are resurrected and born again with Christ. The beautiful prayer for "Thanksgiving Over the Water," in the baptismal liturgy of the *Book of Common Prayer*, expresses the compelling and moving history of water and celebrates it as the great gift it is:

We thank you, Almighty God, for the gift of water. Over it the Holy Spirit moved in the beginning of creation. Through it you led the children of Israel out of their bondage in Egypt into the land of promise. In it your Son Jesus received the baptism of John and was anointed by the Holy Spirit as the Messiah, the Christ, to lead us, through his death and resurrection, from the bondage of sin into everlasting life. (306)

Water is the symbol of God's power to change and transform the world. We may not be able to understand exactly how that happens, but as theologian Gordon Lathrop writes, "One spends one's lifetime learning what the bath has meant."[2]

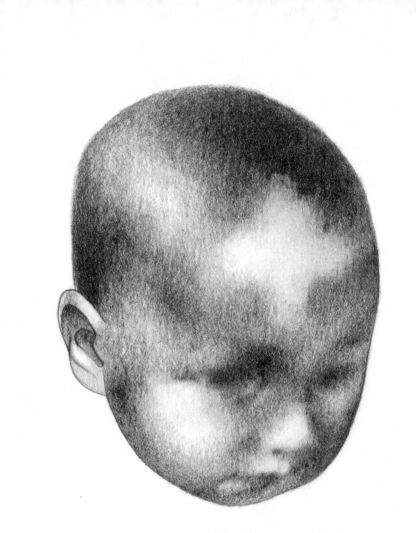

We are anointed with the undeniable love of God.

3

❦

Chrism

. . . marked as Christ's own for ever. Amen.

(*BCP,* 308)

While I was a senior at Virginia Theological Seminary, I took an upper-level Old Testament course taught by Dr. Judy Fentress-Williams. The course had an impressive, official academic title, but was affectionately known by those of us in the class as "Moses Goes to the Movies." We studied the books of Exodus and 1 and 2 Samuel, and compared the biblical texts of the Moses and David narratives to the interpretation of those texts in a wide array of biblical films. One of the scenes from the films that stands out most vividly in my mind is Samuel anointing David with oil, symbolizing his call from God to be the next king of Israel. God chooses David, and David's anointing is the seal of God's call.

At baptism we, too, have been chosen and called by God. Sometimes we are called as young adults or as older adults. Sometimes our parents bring us to the font as infants or young children, as part of our family's collective call to be claimed by Christ.

Unlike the depiction of anointing in the biblical films, when we use chrism at baptism it is not a generous or extravagant pouring of oil over the newly baptized one's head, but a symbolic gesture of sealing a person in the name of the Holy Spirit, just as Jesus was anointed by the Holy Spirit at his baptism. Again, the anointing with chrism is part of the sacrament, the outward and visible sign of the inward anointing we receive by the Holy Spirit. We are anointed as a means of sacramentally connecting us with the anointing of Christ at his baptism.

If the bishop is present at the baptism, the

chrism will be consecrated as part of the service of baptism:

Eternal Father, whose blessed Son was anointed by the Holy Spirit to be the Savior and servant of all, we pray you to consecrate this oil, that those who are sealed with it may share in the royal priesthood of Jesus Christ; who lives and reigns with you and the Holy Spirit, for ever and ever. Amen. (BCP, 307)

If the bishop is not present, the priest uses oil previously consecrated by the bishop.

After baptism the bishop or priest marks the sign of the cross on the person's forehead. Since the second century, chrism has been the sacramental oil used in the service of Holy Baptism. You will find, however, that some clergy who baptize do not use chrism, as they feel that the water of the baptism is theologically enough for the anointing.

You do not have to have chrism; the cross can certainly be signed on the still-wet forehead of the newly baptized. But the use of chrism is an ancient sacramental gesture, and the oil shines through the water and gives the sense of something that will last far beyond the water, which evaporates off the forehead.

As the sign of the cross is marked on our forehead in baptism, we are connected with generations of Christians throughout the centuries. Essentially, we are marking our entire selves as belonging to Christ and to the Body of Christ. This simple, small gesture seals us, marks us—in body, mind, and spirit. The signing of the cross is accompanied by the words "You are sealed by the Holy Spirit in Baptism and marked as Christ's own forever."

During his senior year in high school, our son became seriously ill with a rare blood disorder, and was hospitalized. It was a terrifying time as the doctors informed us that they were running out of options for treatment and there remained only one last treatment to try. We consented to the treatment, and continued our stay at the hospital by our son's bedside.

Our son was very ill. My husband stayed with him during the morning and through lunch. Then I would come in the early afternoon so my husband could go to work, and I would stay the evening and through the night. The medical staff was having no success in bringing down our son's soaring temperature one night, so, at the kind suggestion of the nurses (I think they knew I needed to do something), I was placing cool, wet cloths on our son's forehead to try to make him more comfortable. Our son was too sick to really talk, but I was in active dialogue—sometimes silently, sometimes out loud—talking to and pleading with God throughout the night: Please, God. Please do not let him die. Please, God. Make him well.

At one point in the night, our son softly said, "Mom, put your hand on my forehead and just hold it there." When our children were very young, I would always place my hand on their foreheads when they were not feeling well, just as my mother had done with me.

As I laid my hand on his forehead, our son said, "Mom, thank you for loving me."

I wept almost uncontrollably as I looked at my son's face, with his closed eyes and his lips parched and cracked from the high fever. As my hand lay on his forehead, the words that floated through my mind were those from when our son was baptized, "You are marked as Christ's own forever" (*BCP*, 308). It was at that moment that I felt peace. I felt that no matter what happened, everything was all right. All shall be well and all shall be well, as Julian of Norwich wrote. The next morning the priest from our parish came to the hospital and anointed our son with oil—not chrism, but the healing oil of unction.

We were blessed by the full, if somewhat slow, recovery of our son, but I feel that his illness was one of the pivotal points of my faith journey. It reaffirmed to me the power of the claim that is laid on us with our baptism.

When we gesture with the sign of the cross, as many of us do during worship or our own prayers, we are affirming the sign given to us at our baptism. We are saying, "Yes, I belong to you, Christ." Even the words "in the name of the Father, and of the Son, and of the Holy Spirit," the words we use when making the sign of the cross, have their roots in the ancient baptismal liturgy. With the sign of the cross, we recognize the Trinity—one God, Father, Son, and Holy Spirit; we celebrate our indissoluble connection to the Body of Christ; and we affirm that our baptism has sealed us as belonging to Christ forever.

After her graduation from Kenyon College, when our daughter was living and working in San Francisco, she worked at a preschool for homeless children. These were young children whose parents at best lived in shelters and at worst lived in cars or on the streets. She shared with me at one point the story of a little boy whose behavior was challenging not only to the teachers but to the other children as well. His mother disappeared, and the little boy began to be cared for by his grandfather. His grandfather patiently walked his small grandson to the preschool every morning; before he left him, he would kneel down and make the sign of the cross on the little boy's forehead and give him a hug. The ritual would be repeated at the end of the day. The grandfather would appear, kneel down, and make the sign of the cross on the little boy's forehead, sometimes saying a simple prayer of blessing, and then he would rise, take the little boy's hand in his own, and off they would walk home. My daughter said that the child who had once been so difficult was transformed. Of course it was not just the making of the sign of the cross on his forehead. Obviously the little boy was in a more stable environment and was with someone who cared about him. Still, you cannot help but see the parallels to God, our Father, marking us as his own and reaching out to hold our hands and walk us through the difficult times of our lives. The tiny gesture of a cross signed on our foreheads, either literally or metaphorically, is one that binds us to the One who loves us unconditionally.

With chrism we are anointed with the undeniable love of God.

What is that beautiful thing that just happened?

4

༄

Spirit

You are sealed by the Holy Spirit in Baptism.

(*BCP*, 308)

Listen to the words of poet Mary Oliver in her beautiful poem "At Blackwater Pond":

At Blackwater Pond the tossed waters have settled
after a night of rain.
I dip my cupped hands. I drink
a long time. It tastes
like stone, leaves, fire. It falls cold
into my body, waking the bones. I hear them
deep inside me, whispering
*oh what is that beautiful thing
that just happened?*[3]

In baptism the "beautiful thing" that happens is the Holy Spirit. In baptism water and fire embrace and dance with one another.

This is not a new dance, for the Holy Spirit—the wind from God—swept over the waters in Creation. Just as the creator Spirit transformed the unformed void described in the Book of Genesis, the Holy Spirit transforms our own deep waters, and we, too, are delivered from chaos and void.

It is the Holy Spirit that makes the water more than just water. The outward water pours over our heads, as the Holy Spirit pours inward—over, in, and throughout us. We are infused with Christ's risen existence, receiving the gift of new life through baptism by the Holy Spirit.

For the Holy Spirit is gift, and this gift is offered to everyone through baptism. Peter speaks in the Acts of the Apostles:

And you will receive the gift of the Holy Spirit. For the promise is for you, for your children, and for all who are far away, everyone whom the Lord our God calls to him. (2:38–39)

The Holy Spirit is the gift of God's presence in our lives forever and ever.

The gospels of Matthew, Mark, and Luke tell almost identical stories about what happened that day when Jesus was baptized. They describe the Spirit descending on Jesus like a dove and a voice from heaven proclaiming, "You are my Son, the Beloved; with you I am well pleased."

Recalling the gospel story, the *Book of Common Prayer* also tells us that when Jesus was baptized by John in the River Jordan, Jesus was "anointed by the Holy Spirit as the Messiah, the Christ, to lead us, through his death and resurrection, from the bondage of sin into everlasting life" (306).

We, too, are named and claimed as God's own at baptism. For regardless of our age, whether we are six months old or sixty years old, we are God's children, God's beloved. We are all baptized in the Holy Spirit.

Yet, let us remember that baptism is God's work, not our work. Coming to the font does not decree the Holy Spirit to appear on our demand, to come at this particular time in this particular place. We are the latecomers. The Holy Spirit is there first. God is always already there waiting for us. As Paul wrote in the letter to Titus:

But when the goodness and loving kindness of God our Savior appeared, he saved us, not because of any works of righteousness that we had done, but according to his mercy, through the water of rebirth and renewal by the Holy Spirit. . . . The saying is sure. (3:4–5,8)

The saying is sure.

The Holy Spirit sustains us in that sureness of God's mercy. The real gift of the Holy Spirit is the gift of God's mercy and love. Nothing we do, however righteous or good, earns God's love. God's love is given as pure gift. The Holy Spirit comes as pure gift. The Holy Spirit is the heart of baptism because God's love is at the heart of all sacraments.

Like the Logos, the Holy Spirit exists outside time and space. The Holy Spirit acts in and through the sacrament of baptism but is never bound by the sacrament. The Holy Spirit will not allow itself to be small or to keep an appointment at some hour we try to designate. The Holy Spirit is the essence of wild, mad, beautiful freedom.

The Holy Spirit is not a one-time gift. It is a gift that keeps giving and moving and transforming our lives far beyond the boundaries of the day of our baptism. If we pay attention, we can be forever asking:

oh what is that beautiful thing
that just happened?

We are asked to choose.

5

ॐ

Do You? Will You?

The Candidate for Holy Baptism will now be presented.
(BCP, 301)

Baptism is not a social event or something to be taken lightly, yet it is not something that happens in private or alone. Candidates for Holy Baptism are presented. We cannot present ourselves; we must have someone sponsor us to receive the sacrament of baptism. This is as true for adults as it is for infants and young children. None of us stand alone as Christians—not even at this first moment when we come to the font. Our sponsors stand right beside us and speak for us even before we speak for ourselves.

Sometimes for infants and young children, we use the term "godparents" instead of "sponsors." It is always an honor to be asked to accept the position of godparent, but it also means serious responsibility. Both the parents and the godparents are asked, as part of the liturgy:

Will you be responsible for seeing that the child you present is brought up in the Christian faith and life? (*BCP*, 302)

Whom you select and ask to serve as your child's godparent is a serious decision that needs prayerful reflection by both parents, as well as discussion between parents. Who do you know who takes his or her faith seriously and will also find joy in helping you, as parents, support your child as he or she journeys in faith and life? Who will pray for your child? Who will pray for you as parents? Who will be a joyful witness of your child as he or she grows and matures in faith? Who will be there for you and for your child beyond this one festive day of the service of Holy Baptism? Pray these questions.

The sacrament of Holy Baptism is a worship

service filled with questions. This seems quite fitting because hopefully it is questions that have brought you to the moment of receiving this sacrament and it is questions that will continue to both haunt and enlighten your lifelong journey as a child of God. Love the questions.

The questions of the Examination for Holy Baptism (*BCP*, 302) are questions that move us from darkness to light, from the old life to the new creation:

Do you renounce Satan and the spiritual forces of wickedness that rebel against God?

Do you renounce the evil powers of this world which corrupt and destroy the creatures of God?

Do you renounce all sinful desires that draw you from the love of God?

These questions are rather the showstoppers. We don't talk much about Satan or wickedness or evil powers on a daily basis. We may have a bit more familiarity with our own sinful desires, but all these questions alert us to the drastic step we are taking with baptism: We are committing ourselves to leading a different life. We are choosing whom we will serve. We are called to publicly renounce the darkness in the world and in our lives, renouncing all that draws us away from the love of God. We are also called to affirm all that is light and good:

Do you turn to Jesus Christ and accept him as your Savior?
Do you put your whole trust in his grace and love?
Do you promise to follow and obey him as your Lord?

Darkness and light. Bondage and freedom. Rejection or acceptance. Turning from the old life to a new way. We are given choices in the liturgy, just as we will be given choices throughout our life journeys. We are asked to choose between the darkness and the light. We are asked to be brave enough to renounce the powers of this world and to follow the promise of grace and love offered by Christ.

Everyone in the congregation is asked:

Will you who witness these vows do all in your power to support these persons in their life in Christ? (*BCP,* 303)

The expected answer is:

We will.

That is why it is important for baptism to take place in the congregation where you live and worship. Following Christ is not an easy road; you need the support of fellow sojourners along the path. You want to belong to a community of people who have stood and taken a vow before God to support you in your life in Christ. You want to belong to a community of God's people that will pray the questions with you for a long, long time.

God has placed in the skies the sign of the covenant.

6

ॐ

Covenant

Do you believe . . . ? I believe . . .

(*BCP,* 304)

In baptism God gives and we promise.

With the words of our Baptismal Covenant (*BCP,* 304), we promise what we believe and what we will do because of those beliefs. For those who are too young to make the promises on their own on the day of their baptism, parents, godparents, and all who love these little ones make the promises for them until they grow into the promises and confirm them on their own. On that day of baptism and again on the day of confirmation, we promise to do it all "with God's help" (*BCP*, 304). After all, Christianity is not a self-help program; we recognize and name up front that it is God who makes all things possible.

What does the word *covenant* mean? If you look it up in the dictionary, you find this definition: "a binding and solemn agreement made by two or more individuals to do or keep from doing a specified thing."[4] The ancient meaning of *covenant* is "a bond that seals the relationship between two parties." No concept is more central to Israel than that of covenant. The very event that established Israel as God's people focused on the covenant Moses made for the people with God on Mount Sinai. These words from Exodus tell us about the covenant made that day:

You have seen what I did to the Egyptians, and how I bore you on eagles' wings and brought you to myself. Now therefore, if you obey my voice and keep my covenant, you shall be my treasured possession out of all the peoples. (19:4–5)

The Great Vigil of Easter (*BCP*, 285), a church service that often includes Holy Baptism and always includes the words of our Baptismal Covenant, features a reading from the Book of Genesis about the covenant made between Noah and God: After the flood, when the waters recede, God establishes a covenant with Noah and the people using the outward sacrament of a rainbow. After that scripture reading, we pray this collect from the *Book of Common Prayer*:

Almighty God, you have placed in the skies the sign of your covenant with all living things: Grant that we, who are saved through water and the Spirit, may worthily offer to you our sacrifice of thanksgiving; through Jesus Christ our Lord. (289)

God gives, and we promise.

God begins the action by calling and acting, and then God waits. We, just as all called people throughout history, must choose to respond to God's call. The good news is that God is almost irresistible. As Augustine wrote, "Thou hast made us for thyself, and our hearts are restless till they find their rest in thee." We, as human beings, have a deep longing to hear God's call. We yearn to be in covenant relationship with God. It is almost as if it is part of our DNA. Yes, God, I'm listening. What will you have me do? What will you have me become? I will, with your help, God.

God keeps his promise of the new covenant through Jesus Christ; we keep our promise by being baptized into the Christian community. But even after baptism, there will be times when we ignore God and do not respond. After all, we are fully human. The good news is that our response has nothing to do with God's presence in our lives, for God is always with us. As Paul wrote:

For I am convinced that neither death, nor life, nor angels, nor rulers, nor things present, nor things to come, nor powers, nor height, nor depth, nor anything else in all creation, will be able to separate us from the love of God in Christ Jesus our Lord. (Romans 8:38–39)

The words of the Baptismal Covenant are witness to our need for God. We make this covenant, this promise of our beliefs and commitment, in public so that all may hear the ongoing transformation that is happening in our lives through Jesus Christ. We make this commitment in public so that all may hear that we can believe or do these things only "with God's help." The words of the Baptismal Covenant simply serve as a reminder of all God has done for us.

The covenant means we continue to remember. Baptism helps us remember who we are and whose we are. Someone far greater than us has named us and claimed us and will always and forever sustain us.

Baptism is not just a rational decision to accept Christ and Christian teachings. God's call evokes a far deeper promise and commitment with us and within us. The new covenant with Jesus Christ has been written not on tablets of stone but directly on our hearts. The sacrament of baptism is the Spirit-sealed promise of an ongoing and ever-continuing covenant with God. God's covenant is this: Baptism is once and for all time. We are sealed by the Holy Spirit and marked as Christ's own forever, and that seal is indissoluble.

Throughout our worldly lives, God challenges us to "choose this day whom you will serve" (Joshua 24:15). It is up to us to remember each day what we promise to believe, to remember what we promise to do, and to remember who it is that has set the rainbow in the sky (Genesis 9:12–16). It is up to us to remember our baptism and to be grateful for the gift of a covenant sealed with the indissoluble love of God.

Baptism is an act of community.

7

৯৯

Communion

Keep them in the faith and communion
of your holy Church. (*BCP,* 305)

Sacraments involve and
affect the whole Church. Baptism is no exception. We
do baptism together as a community in the Church.
Baptism brings us into "common union"—or communion—both with God and with one another.

Not long ago private baptisms were popular,
even the norm; however, today our theology of baptism stresses, as stated in the *Book of Common Prayer,*
that "Holy Baptism is full initiation by water and
the Holy Spirit into Christ's Body the Church"
(298). Baptism brings a child or an adult into the

family of God. Even though we often gather aunts, uncles, grandparents, friends, and others for this joyful celebration, the group of people at the heart of this sacrament is not only our genetic family but also our Church family.

Baptism is an act of community, not an act of individualism. We do not each receive a tiny, individual serving of the Holy Spirit engraved with our own name, just as the Eucharist is not our own personal Happy Meal. The great beauty and joy of baptism and of all sacraments is that we share, we come together and become part of the one Spirit given to God's people as a group, as the great communion of saints.

Baptism is a sacramental action of welcome into the Body of Christ. At some parishes the celebrant purposefully meets those being baptized at the church door, to symbolically communicate the importance of their entrance into the household of God and the community of faith. It is a symbolic way of saying: "This is your home now. This is your family. Come in."

The community's love is offered and the

newly baptized are welcomed to share in the responsibilities of the community. When a baby is baptized, just as with older children and adults, the entire community is present, not just the parents and godparents. The whole community accepts the role of providing guidance as the child grows in and into her or his Christian faith. The sacrament of baptism affects the one being baptized and all those who are present. It is through the promises of those who are present that the newly baptized "grow into the full stature of Christ" (*BCP*, 302).

Baptism in community is no casual choice; it is profoundly important. It is no accident that we all join together in saying the Baptismal Covenant, committing the entire gathered communion to Christ. It is no accident that our prayers are corporate prayers: Lord, hear *our* prayer.

Regardless of our age, initiation into our Christian faith is not a single worship service, not a lone Sunday morning event. Faith is a lifelong process of learning and growth. The communion in the household of God really begins before the moment of baptism; all that comes before is what draws one to the font in the first place.

But the sacrament of baptism is how we say *yes* to God. God has already been reaching out for us; coming to the font is our way of reaching back and joining hands with all those who are part of our common life in Christ.

As evidenced in both the early Church, described in the Acts of the Apostles, and today's contemporary Church, the purpose of Christian communion is to nurture, challenge, and deepens one's faith, both individually and collectively. It is through this collective and shared communion with one another that we as Christians develop our vision, mission, values, and identity as children of God. Because our growth as Christians, as people exploring the depths of our faith, happens in this shared communion, the sacrament of baptism needs to happen in the context of the sacramental community.

Through this communion we remind one another of our real identity in the world.

For we are not just in communion with one

another in the church, we are also in communion with God and with Christ Jesus. Presbyterian minister William Fogelman, writing in the journal *Interpretation,* shares that Martin Luther is said to have reminded himself in times of despair, "I *am* baptized."[5]

This simply stated awareness of his true identity, his *Christian* identity, apparently brought Luther to his senses, restoring balance and proper perspective to the situation. This might be an excellent touchstone prayer for any of us on those days when we feel more frustrated than delighted, more overwhelmed than encouraged. Well, if nothing else seems to be going right today, at least I am baptized. With that we are saying that we are part of something so much larger, so much deeper, so much richer than ourselves.

Even when we forget our true selves and the true meaning of our lives in this world, our communion with one another reminds us of our communion with God.

The communion of baptism celebrates relationship. Once baptized, we will never be without family.

Our witness will be dazzlingly bright.

8

༄

Witness

Send them into the world in witness to your love.

(*BCP*, 306)

Baptism is not the end of our faith journey, but the beginning.

The witness begins with a small point of light. Like John the Baptist, in John 1:7, "He came as a witness to testify to the light." With our baptism we, too, come as witnesses to testify to the light.

After our baptism the priest lights a small baptismal candle from the bright light of the paschal candle. The large paschal candle, which each year enters the church with the celebration of Easter, represents Christ as the light of the world. We receive our baptismal candle as a symbol that Christ's light has come into our own life through our baptism. We receive the candle as a symbol that we are now chosen to carry Christ's light out into the world. We receive the candle as a symbol of moving from darkness into the light and of being commissioned by God to lead others from darkness to light. To paraphrase D. T. Niles, this is witness: one beggar telling another beggar where to find bread.

Through baptism we join the work of the Church—sharing the gospel, the good news, about what God has done in Jesus Christ. Martin Luther wrote:

If, then, the holy sacrament of baptism is a matter so great, gracious, and full of comfort, we should diligently see to it that we ceaselessly, joyfully, and from the heart thank, praise, and honor God for it. . . . The whole world was, and still is, full of baptism and the grace of God.[6]

What a beautiful image that is: a world full of baptism, a world full of the grace of God. It is no surprise that we want to share with others all this that comforts, brings joy, and showers God's grace upon us. Baptism is the beginning of our commission to go into the world and live as Christians. We begin our journey or, perhaps more accurately, we now consciously and mindfully continue our journey, taking steps toward living out our Baptismal Covenant.

Even though the phrase has been trivialized by overmarketing, we need to ask ourselves seriously, "What would Jesus do?"—and then do just that. Or try to do that. We are called to witness, and we can all do something. It is not just about the work in the Church within a religious context. Our baptismal covenant is lived out in how we walk through our everyday lives; not just in the church, but at the grocery store, in the classroom, while driving along the interstate.

Age is irrelevant to our witness. The smile of a small child might be all that is needed to touch the heart of someone who is struggling with depression or the loneliness of old age. Even those who, because of physical disabilities, are homebound can still pray. We can pray from our beds or we can make phone calls, write notes, or send e-mails. Witnessing is reaching out to others, especially to those who feel that no one cares.

God has blessed every one of us with gifts. Jean Vanier, the founder of the L'Arche community, where adults with physical and mental disabilities and those without disabilities live together in shared community, told this story as part of his meditations at the 1998 Lambeth Conference. It is the story of a family with a mentally retarded child; they had just returned from attending a magnificent baptismal worship service:

And the uncle of the little boy said to the mother (and the little boy was nearby) "Wasn't it a beautiful liturgy? The only thing that's sad is that he understood nothing." The little boy looked at his mother, with tears in his eyes, and said, "Don't worry mummy, Jesus loves me as I am." [7]

The little boy in Vanier's meditation was a witness for God's love with his simple yet profound words: "Jesus loves me as I am." By our baptism we are called to share with others that Jesus loves us all as we are, regardless of our disabilities or our broken-ness. By our baptism we are called to live for Christ and to live strengthened by the abundance of Christ's love.

The earliest Christians had no doubts about the purpose of their lives or their identity as disciples. It is still true that we learn what it means to be a Christian simply by being one, by living as one, by continuing to reflect on what it means and how to act on that meaning. Even though the sign of the cross made on our foreheads in baptism initially marks us as a Christian, in all the years that follow, we continue to retrace the imprint of that cross, marking ourselves and our lives as we live into our faith.

It is not a simple, easy, linear journey. There are twists and turns and certainly switchbacks along the way. For some of us, the challenge is in trying to reconcile the past with the present of our lives. A powerful scene in Toni Morrison's novel *Beloved* relates the horrific effects of slavery. Sethe, a woman who has escaped slavery but has not escaped the memories that continue to haunt and terrorize her, is told by the freed slave Paul: "Me and you, we got more yesterday than anybody. We need some kind of tomorrow."[8]

As Christians we believe that God, through Christ, has given us the tomorrow that makes it possible for us to endure all that happened to us yesterday. We affirm that each Sunday at the Eucharist when we say: *Christ has died* (yes, yesterday was pretty terrible); *Christ is risen* (but things have turned around now); *Christ will come again* (Oh, what a great tomorrow it will be!). With the sacrament of baptism, we are connected to Christ and we receive the power and hope for all our tomorrows. It is this hope we are called to remember for ourselves and to share with others.

Sacraments are not passive. Sacraments are not just something we are presented and we receive. Sacraments charge our souls and send us into the world—to act, to witness, to celebrate, to share.

We are called into the world to witness to the love of God. We are called to break out of the dark and binding cocoon of our self-centeredness and to spread our unique and colorful wings, testifying to the resurrection that frees us and the grace that blesses us. We are called to let the light of our baptismal candles shine out into the world. They are just small lights, but if we shine them together, our witness will be dazzlingly bright.

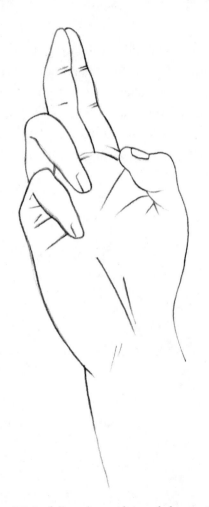

We joyfully welcome the newly baptized.

9

ༀ

Welcome!

We receive you into the household of God.

(*BCP*, 308)

Our *Book of Common Prayer* has a rather sedate and dignified welcome for those who have just received the sacrament of Holy Baptism. The celebrant says, "Let us welcome the newly baptized" (308), and then concludes with a prayer.

Now, there is nothing wrong with that welcoming sentence or with that order of service, but if we really believe in the power and joy of the sacrament of Holy Baptism, we might try a more celebratory approach for the conclusion of the service.

When our family was living in Memphis, Tennessee, and attending Calvary Episcopal Church, a vibrant downtown parish under the leadership of the Reverend Doug Bailey, one of my favorite moments was at the conclusion of the baptismal service, when Doug, holding the newly baptized baby in his arms or holding the hand of an older person, would face the congregation and say, always with an enormous smile: "Christians, meet our newest Christian."

The congregation would always burst into applause, and Doug would process up and back down the center aisle with this "newest Christian" in his arms or walking by his side. It was always a moment when everyone in the congregation, like Doug, was grinning from ear to ear. It was also a moment when you felt overjoyed to be named and claimed as a Christian and to be part of the community of Christians.

For you never just watch a baptism; you are always a part of the sacramental moment, and that is what makes it so delightful. What a joy it is to celebrate being part of the community of God's people welcoming a new child of God to the community.

That is why we join with those who are committing themselves to Christ and always say together our Baptismal Covenant.

We are not only greeting a new Christian— *Welcome! Welcome! Welcome to the Body of Christ!*— we are also remembering our own reception of the sacrament of new birth. We remember our baptism so that we, too, continue in our life of grace. We remember our baptism so that our hearts might always be inquiring and discerning so that we might always have the courage to persevere and the spirit to know and love God.

But mostly we joyfully welcome the newly baptized to join in the everlasting celebration of the joy and wonder of God's work in the world.

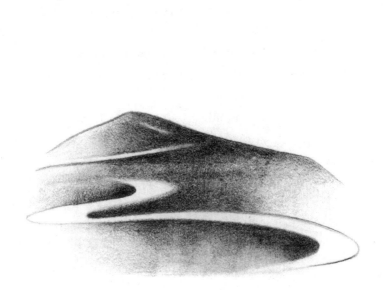

We have journeyed to this day of our baptism.

10

༄

Remember
Your Baptism

$\mathbf{B}$aptism is completely free, but it will cost you everything.

Yes, baptism is free. You don't rent the church or pay the priest or purchase the chrism—it is pure gift. It is not only pure gift from a parish, it is pure gift from God. On the day of your baptism, you say *yes* to God, and God says *yes* right back to you, in the beauty and power of all those outward and visible signs. But God's grace, freely given, has been with us long before the moment of our baptism. The reality is that God actually says *yes* to each of us from the moment we are formed in the womb, from the microsecond we are created in God's image. Maybe even before that.

Saying *yes* to God and to baptism does not end our journey but starts it from a new place. We have journeyed, some of us longer than others, to this day of our baptism, but the *yes* keeps on working. Designating the word *yes* as a verb is grammatically incorrect, but a correct image for our faith journey. Our baptismal *yes* is an action verb that keeps acting throughout our lives, sometimes seen and sometimes unseen, to touch us and to touch the lives of others. *Yes* is like one of those verbs you study in biblical Greek class, those verbs that really have no beginning and no end; they just keep moving and working and going. The action is continuous and continual. *Yes!*

Consciously or unconsciously, everything changes with our baptism. It is through remembering that we begin to reflect on the transformation given by this sacrament.

When we begin to recognize what it means to be marked as Christ's own forever, as we begin to live into the fullness and deepness of Christ and of that forever, it is enough to take our breath away.

Still, we sometimes mistakenly think that everything will be easier in our lives. We've chosen Christ, so now we will live in the world as Christ's chosen ones and our lives will be perfect. Only good things will happen to us, and we will be rewarded with all our heart's desires. Open the Bible at almost any point and you will quickly see that this line of thinking is not new, but it also does not go very far, in scripture or in real life. We remember our baptism and begin to understand that it offers us comfort in the wilderness but it will not prevent us from experiencing the wilderness.

When we fully recognize that we are marked as Christ's own forever, as we begin to live into the fullness and deepness of Christ and of that forever, we are faced with making choices that will not always route us down the easiest or most comfortable path. We remember our baptism and choose.

If anything, claiming our Christian name and identity makes our life journey more difficult. Now we travel the journey with an awareness of who we really are and who we are called by Christ to be. It is never easy to live a life of authenticity and credibility. Yes, baptism is completely free, but it will cost you everything.

Remember your baptism.

Notes

1. In Kurt Niederwimmer, *The Didache: A Commentary*, Linda M. Maloney, trans.; Harold W. Attridge, ed. (Minneapolis: Fortress Press, 1998), 125.

2. Gordon W. Lathrop, *Holy Things: A Liturgical Theology* (Minneapolis: Fortress Press, 1993), 60.

3. Mary Oliver, "At Blackwater Pond," in *New and Selected Poems* (Boston: Beacon Press, 1992), 226.

4. *Webster's New World Dictionary of the American Language*, David B. Guralnik, ed. (New York: Simon and Schuster, 1984), 326.

5. William J. Fogelman, "Romans 6:3–14," in *Interpretation 47* (July 1993), 296.

6. Martin Luther, "The Holy and Blessed Sacrament of Baptism," in *Luther's Works: Word and Sacrament*, volume 35, E. Theodore Bachmann, ed. (Philadelphia: Fortress Press, 1955), 42.

7. Jean Vanier, "Vigil of Meditation, Prayer and Washing of Feet I," in *The Official Report of the Lambeth Conference 1998* (Harrisburg, PA: Morehouse, 1998), 459–460.

8. Toni Morrison, *Beloved* (New York: Plume, 1988), 288.